COPY RIGHT 2020 BY TAMOH ART PUBLISHING
ALL RIGHTS SERVICES ARE RESERVED

HOW TO PRAY
IN ISLAM
BOOK FOR MUSLIMS
ADULTS AND KIDS

67 pages 8 x 10 in

1/Prayer in Islam:
From page n° 2 till page n° 52

2/ Ablution in Islam:
From page n° 54 till page n° 66

This book belongs to:

....

....

« Bismi llàhi rrahmàni rrahime »
In the name of Allah, Most Gracious, Most Merciful.

FIRST OF ALL:
If you want to pray, you should keep yourself in state
of clean and pure. And so as to be so,
you have to perform ablution.
"Prayer without ablution is invalid »

The five daily prayers in Islam:

Prayers	Raka-ahs	Recitation	Time of Prayers
AL-FAJR	2 rakaahs	Two loudly Raka-ahs + Tashahhud + Abrahamic Prayer + Salam Aalyekoume.	Dawn, before sunrise.
ADDOUHUR	4 rakaahs	Two silent Raka-ahs + Tashahhud + Two silent Raka-ahs + Tashahhud + Abrahamic Prayer + Salam Aalyekoume.	Midday, after the sun passes its highest.
AL-ASER	4 rakaahs	Two silent Raka-ahs + Tashahhud + Two silent Raka-ahs + Tashahhud + Abrahamic Prayer + Salam Aalyekoume.	The late part of the afternoon
AL-MAGHEB	3 rakaahs	Two loudly Raka-ahs + Tashahhud + One silent Raka-ah + Tashahhud + Abrahamic Prayer + Salam Aalyekoume.	Just after sunset.
AL-AISHAA	4 rakaahs	Two loudly Raka-ahs + Tashahhud + Two silent Raka-ahs + Tashahhud + Abrahamic Prayer + Salam Aalyekoume.	Between sunset and midnight.

N.B. : Muslim **women/girl**s have to recite all quranic verses silently while praying.

This is the illustration of « S a l a h A D D U H E R » with four silent « raka-ahs"

First, stand up, your face towards the KEBLA, MECCA

Then, always start with "Bismillaah »: in the name of Allah.

You should have the intention to pray and then say:

الله أكبر الله أكبر

«Allàhou akbar, allàhou akbar. »

Allah is Great, Allah is Great

أشهد أن لا إلاه إلا الله

« Ashehadou anna là ilàha illa llàh »

I bear witness that there is no god but Allah

وأشهد أن محمدا عبده و رسوله

« Wa ashehadou anna mohammadane abdouhou
 wa rassoulouhou »

**And I bear witness that Muhammad is His slave
and Prophet**

حي على الصلاة حي على الفلاح

« hayya a-alà ssalàti, hayya a-alà lfalàhi »

Come to prayer, come to success

قد قامت الصلاة

« Qade qàmati ssalàtou »

Prayer has been established,

الله أكبر الله أكبر

«allàhou akbar , allàhou akbar. »

Allah is Great, Allah is Great

لا إلاه إلا الله

« là ilàha illa llàh »

there is no god but Allah.

The First « RAKA-AH »

Start your prayer by your first « RAKA-AH », and say:

الله أكبر

« Allàhou akbar »

Allah is Great

- Look the following image -

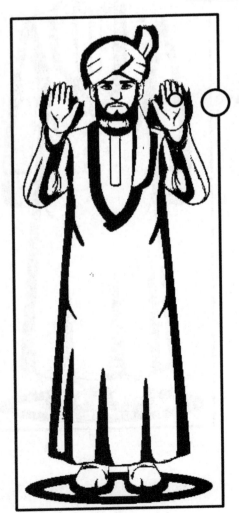

الله أكبر
« Allàhou akbar »
Allah is Great

Then, recite silently surah Al-Fatiha:

بسم الله الرحمان الرحيم

« Bismillàhi rrahmàni rrahime »

In the name of Allah, Most Gracious, Most Merciful.

الْحَمْدُ لِلَّهِ رَبِّ الْعَالَمِينَ

« Alhamdou lilàhi rabbi al-a-alamine »

Praise be to Allah, the Cherisher and Sustainer of the worlds,

الرَّحْمٰنِ الرَّحِيمِ

« Arrahmàni rrahiime »

Most Gracious, Most Merciful,

مَالِكِ يَوْمِ الدِّينِ

« Màliki yawemi ddiine »

Master of the Day of Judgment.

إِيَّاكَ نَعْبُدُ وَإِيَّاكَ نَسْتَعِينُ

« Iyyàka na-aboudo wa iyyàka nasta-ine »

Thee do we worship, and Thine aid we seek.

اهْدِنَا الصِّرَاطَ الْمُسْتَقِيمَ

« Ihdina ssiràta almoustaqime »

Show us the straight way,

صِرَاطَ الَّذِينَ أَنْعَمْتَ عَلَيْهِمْ غَيْرِ الْمَغْضُوبِ عَلَيْهِمْ وَلَا الضَّالِّينَ. امين.

« Siràta lladina ane-ameta alayehime, ghayri almaghdoubi
a-alayehime, wala ddàliine. Amine »

**The way of those on whom Thou hast bestowed Thy Grace,
those whose (portion) is not wrath, and who go not astray.**
Amine.

بإسم الله الرحمان الرحيم

« Bismillàhi rrahmàni rrahime »

In the Name of Allâh, the Most Beneficent, the Most Merciful.

قُلْ هُوَ اللَّهُ أَحَدٌ

« Qoul houa llàhou ahade »

Say "Allâh is (the) One

اللَّهُ الصَّمَدُ

« Allàhou ssamade »

The Self-Sufficient Master

لَمْ يَلِدْ وَلَمْ يُولَدْ

« Lame yalide walame youlade »

"He begets not, nor was He begotten.

وَلَمْ يَكُنْ لَهُ كُفُوًا أَحَدٌ

« Walame yakoune lahou koufou-ane ahade »

And there is none co-equal or comparable unto Him.

Then, say: :

الله أكبر

« Allàhou akbar »

Allah is Great

And, do as the following image:

Then, say 3 times :

سبحان ربي العظيم

Subhaana rabiyya-al-addime » :

Glory be to my God

Then, standing upright again and saying:

سمع الله لمن حمده /1

"Sami-a allàhou liman hamidah"

Allah listens to those who praise Him

ربنا و لك الحمد /2

« Rabbanà walaka lhamde »

Praise be to our God

Then, say:

الله أكبر :

« Allàhou akbar »

Allah is Great

While prostrating, you have to say 3 times :

سبحان ربي الأعلى

"Subhàna rabiyya-al-alà"

Glory to my God

1/ Raising the head and saying:

الله أكبر

"Allàhou akbar"
Allah is Great

2/ Then, say a request such as :

اللهم إغفر لي و إرحمني

« Làhoumma ighfir li warhamni »
My God, forgive me and have mercy on me

1/ Then slowly bending down to prostrate and saying:

الله أكبر

"Allàhou akbar"

Allah is Great

2/ Once again, while prostrating you have to say 3 times :

سبحان ربي الأعلى

"Subhana rabiyya-al-alà"

Glory to my God

The second « RAKA-AH »

Then, start your second « RAKA-AH » by saying:

الله أكبر

« Allàhou akbar »

Allah is Great

- Look at the following image -

Then, recite once again silently surah Al-Fatiha:

بسم الله الرحمان الرحيم
«Bismillaahi rrahmàni rrahime »
In the name of Allah, Most Gracious, Most Merciful.

الْحَمْدُ لِلَّهِ رَبِّ الْعَالَمِينَ
« Alhamdou lilàhi rabbi al-a-alamine »
Praise be to Allah, the Cherisher and Sustainer of the worlds,

الرَّحْمَٰنِ الرَّحِيمِ
« Arrahmàni rrahime »
Most Gracious, Most Merciful,

مَالِكِ يَوْمِ الدِّينِ
« Màliki yawemi ddine »
Master of the Day of Judgment.

إِيَّاكَ نَعْبُدُ وَإِيَّاكَ نَسْتَعِينُ
« Iyyàka na-boudo wa iyyàka nasta-ine »
Thee do we worship, and Thine aid we seek.

اهْدِنَا الصِّرَاطَ الْمُسْتَقِيمَ
« Ihdina ssiràta almoustaqime »
Show us the straight way,

«صِرَاطَ الَّذِينَ أَنْعَمْتَ عَلَيْهِمْ غَيْرِ الْمَغْضُوبِ عَلَيْهِمْ وَلَا الضَّالِّينَ. امين.
« Siràta lladina ane-ameta alayehime, ghayri almaghdoubi
a-alayehime, wala ddàliine. Amine »
**The way of those on whom Thou hast bestowed Thy Grace,
those whose (portion) is not wrath, and who go not astray.**
Amine.

After finishing Surah AL FATIHA, recite silently any verse from the Quran: For example, Surah An-Nas

قُلْ أَعُوذُ بِرَبِّ النَّاسِ

« Qoule a-oudou birabbi nnàsi »

« Say: I seek refuge with (Allâh) the Lord of mankind, »

مَلِكِ النَّاسِ

« Malki nnàsi »

« The King of mankind »

إِلَهِ النَّاسِ

« Ilàhi nnàsi »

« The Ilâh (God) of mankind, »

مِنْ شَرِّ الْوَسْوَاسِ الْخَنَّاسِ

« Mine charri lwaswàsi lkhannàsi »

« From the evil of the whisperer who Withdraws (from his whispering in one's heart after one remembers Allâh). »

الَّذِي يُوَسْوِسُ فِي صُدُورِ النَّاسِ

« Alladii youwaswisou fi soudouri nnàsi »

« Who whispers in the breasts of mankind. »

مِنَ الْجِنَّةِ وَالنَّاسِ

« Mina ljinnati wa nnàssi »

« Of jinn and mankind. »

Then, say: :

الله أكبر

« Allàhou akbar »

Allah is Great

And, do as the following image:

Then, say 3 times :

سبحان ربي العظيم

''Subhàna rabiyya-al-addime » :

Glory be to my God

Then, standing upright again and saying:

١/ سمع الله لمن حمده
"Samia-a allàhou liman hamidah"
Allah listens to those who praise Him

٢/ ربنا و لك الحمد
« Rabbana walak alhamde »
Praise be to our God

Then, say:

الله أكبر :

« Allàhou akbar »

Allah is Great

While prostrating, you have to say 3 times :

سبحان ربي الأعلى
"Subhàna rabiyya-al-alà"
Glory to my God

1/ Raising the head and saying:

الله أكبر

"Allàhou akbar"
Allah is Great

2/ Then, say a request such as :

اللهم إغفر لي و إرحمني

« Làhoumma ighfir li wa rhamni »
My God, forgive me and have mercy on me

1/ Then slowly bending down to prostrate and saying:

الله أكبر

"Allàhou akbar"

Allah is Great

2/ Once again, while prostrating you have to say 3 times :

سبحان ربي الأعلى

Subhàna rabiyya-al-alà"

Glory to my God

Raising your head and saying:

الله أكبر

"Allàhou akbar"

Allah is Great

Then, you sit on your knees to say the tashahhud while moving your finger of your right hand:
<u>Recite</u> **"tashahhud"**
as written in the following page

Tashahhud:

التحيات لله و الصلوات و الطيبات،

« Attahiyàtou lillàh wa ssalawàtou wa ttayibàte »

All compliments, prayers and pure words are due to Allaah.

السلام عليك أيها النبي ، و رحمة الله و بركاته

«Assalàmou alayeka ayouha nnabi wa rahmatou llàhi wa barakàtouhou »

Peace be upon you, O Prophet, and the mercy of Allaah and His blessings.

السلام علينا و على عباد الله الصالحين،

« Assalàmou alayenà wa alà ibàdi llàhi sàlihina »

Peace be upon us and upon the righteous slaves of Allaah.

أشهد أن لا إله إلا الله،

« Achehadou anna là ilàha illa llàh »

I bear witness that there is no god except Allaah

.و أشهد أن محمدا عبده و رسوله

«Wa achehadou anna mouhammadane abedouhou wa rasoulouhou »

and I bear witness that Muhammad is His slave and Messenger

After finishing the the Tashahhud, then start the third « RAKA-AH », almost like the previous « RAKA-AH ».

The difference between the two previous « Raka-ahs » (the first and the second « RAKA-AH »)
and the following « raka-ah »
is that you have not to recite anything after finishing Surah AL FATIHA.

It's very important to say that the tashahhud is to be recited after finishing the second Raka-ah of each prayer during the day.

So, this is the illustration of the third « RAKA-AH »

Then, start your third « RAKAAH » by saying:

الله أكبر

« Allàhou akbar »

Allah is Great

- Look at the following image -

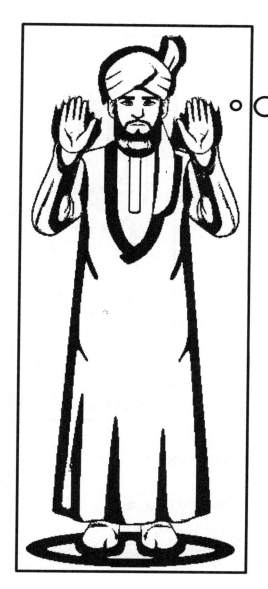

Then, recite again silently surah Al-Fatiha:

بسم الله الرحمان الرحيم
« Bismillàhi rrahmani rrahime »
In the name of Allah, Most Gracious, Most Merciful.

الْحَمْدُ لِلَّهِ رَبّ الْعَالَمِينَ
« Alhamdou lilàhi rabbi al-a-alamine »
Praise be to Allah, the Cherisher and Sustainer of the worlds,

الرَّحْمٰنِ الرَّحِيمِ
« Arrahmàni rrahime »
Most Gracious, Most Merciful,

مَالِكِ يَوْمِ الدّينِ
« Màliki yawemi ddine »
Master of the Day of Judgment.

إِيَّاكَ نَعْبُدُ وَإِيَّاكَ نَسْتَعِينُ
« Iyyàka na-aboudo wa iyyàka nasta-ine »
Thee do we worship, and Thine aid we seek.

اهْدِنَا الصّرَاطَ الْمُسْتَقِيمَ
« Ihdina ssiràta almoustaqime »
Show us the straight way,

صِرَاطَ الَّذِينَ أَنْعَمْتَ عَلَيْهِمْ غَيْرِ الْمَغْضُوبِ عَلَيْهِمْ وَلَا الضَّالِّينَ. امين.
« Siràta lladina ane-ameta alayehime, ghayri almaghdoubi
alayehime, wala ddàliine. Amine »
**The way of those on whom Thou hast bestowed Thy Grace,
those whose (portion) is not wrath, and who go not astray.**
Amine.

Then, say: :

الله أكبر

« Allàhou akbar »

Allah is Great

And, do as the following image:

Then, say 3 times :

سبحان ربي العظيم
« Subhàna rabiyya-al-addime » :
Glory be to my God

Then, standing upright again and saying:

سمع الله لمن حمده

"Sami-a allàhou liman hamidah"

Allah listens to those who praise Him

ربنا و لك الحمد

« Rabbanà walak alhamde »

Praise be to our God

Then, say:

الله أكبر :

« Allàhou akbar »

Allah is Great

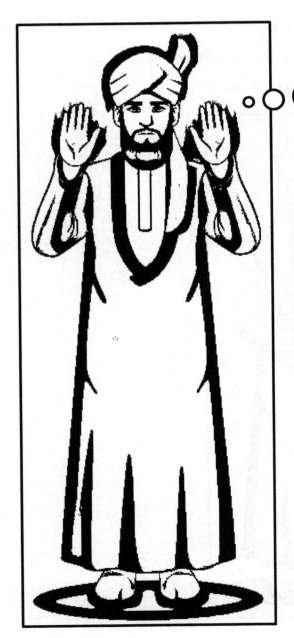

While prostrating, you have to say 3 times :

سبحان ربي الأعلى

"Subhàna rabiyya-al-alà"

Glory to my God

1/ Raising the head and saying:

الله أكبر
"Allàhou akbar"
Allah is Great

2/ Then, say a request such as :

اللهم إغفر لي و إرحمني
« Làhoumma ighfir li wa rhamni »
My God, forgive me and have mercy on me

1/ Then slowly bending down to prostrate and saying:

الله أكبر

"Allàhou akbar"

Allah is Great

2/Once again, while prostrating you have to say 3 times :

سبحان ربي الأعلى

"Subhàna rabiyya-al-alà"

Glory to my God

<u>This is the illustration of the fouth « RAKA-AH »</u>

Then, start your fourth « RAKAAH » by saying:

الله أكبر

« Allàhou akbar »

Allah is Great

- Look the following image -

Then, recite again silently surah Al-Fatiha:

بسم الله الرحمان الرحيم
« Bismillàhi rrahmàni rrahime »
In the name of Allah, Most Gracious, Most Merciful.

الْحَمْدُ لِلَّهِ رَبِّ الْعَالَمِينَ
« Alhamdou lilàhi rabbi al-a-alamine »
Praise be to Allah, the Cherisher and Sustainer of the worlds,

الرَّحْمَٰنِ الرَّحِيمِ
« Arrahmàni rrahime »
Most Gracious, Most Merciful,

مَالِكِ يَوْمِ الدِّينِ
« Màliki yawemi ddine »
Master of the Day of Judgment.

إِيَّاكَ نَعْبُدُ وَإِيَّاكَ نَسْتَعِينُ
« Iyàka na-aboudo wa iyàka nasta-ine »
Thee do we worship, and Thine aid we seek.

اهْدِنَا الصِّرَاطَ الْمُسْتَقِيمَ
« Ihdina siràta almoustaqime »
Show us the straight way,

صِرَاطَ الَّذِينَ أَنْعَمْتَ عَلَيْهِمْ غَيْرِ الْمَغْضُوبِ عَلَيْهِمْ وَلَا الضَّالِّينَ. امين.
« Siràta lladina ane-ameta alayehime, ghayri almaghdoubi
alayehime, wala dàliine. Amine »
**The way of those on whom Thou hast bestowed Thy Grace,
those whose (portion) is not wrath, and who go not astray.**
Amine.

Then, say: :

الله أكبر

« Allàhou akbar »

Allah is Great

And, do as in the following image:

Then, say 3 times :

سبحان ربي العظيم

"Subhàna rabiyya-al-addime » :

Glory be to my God

Then, standing upright again and saying:

1/ سمع الله لمن حمده
"Sami-a allàhou limane hamidah"
Allah listens to those who praise Him

2/ ربنا و لك الحمد
« Rabbanà walaka lhamde »
Praise be to our God

Then, say:

الله أكبر :

« Allàhou akbar »

Allah is Great

2/ While prostrating, you have to say 3 times :

سبحان ربي الأعلى

"Subhàna rabiyya-al-ahlà"
Glory to my God

"Subhàna rabiyya-al-ahlà"

1/ Raising the head and saying:

الله أكبر

"Allàhou akbar"

Allah is Great

2/ Then, say a request such as :

اللهم إغفر لي و إرحمني

« Làhoumma ighfir li wa rhamni »

My God, forgive me and have mercy on me

1/ Then slowly bending down to prostrate and saying:

الله أكبر

"Allàhou akbar"

Allah is Great

2/ Once again, while prostrating you have to say 3 times :

سبحان ربي الأعلى

"Subhàna rabiyya-al-alà"

Glory to my God

1/ Raising the head and saying:

الله أكبر

"Allàhou akbar"

Allah is Great

2/ Then, you sit on your knees and while moving
The finger of your right hand, say both the "tashahhud"
and "Abrahamic Prayer"
as written in the following page

Tashahhud and Abrahamic Prayer:

التحيات لله و الصلوات و الطيبات،

« Attahiyàtou lillàh wa ssalawàtou wa ttayibaate »

All compliments, prayers and pure words are due to Allaah.

السلام عليك أيها النبي ، و رحمة الله و بركاته

«Assalàmou alayeka ayouha nnabi wa rahmatou llàhi wa barakàtouhou »

Peace be upon you, O Prophet, and the mercy of Allaah and His blessings.

السلام علينا و على عباد الله الصالحين،

« Assalàmou alayenà wa alà ibàdi llàhi sàlihina »

Peace be upon us and upon the righteous slaves of Allaah.

أشهد أن لا إله إلا الله،

« Achehadou anna là ilàha illa llàh »

I bear witness that there is no god except Allaah

.و أشهد أن محمدا عبده و رسوله

«Wa achehadou anna mouhammadane abedouhou wa rasoulouhou »

and I bear witness that Muhammad is His slave and Messenger.

اللهم صلي على محمد و على آل محمد

« Allahoumma salli alà mouhammadine wa alà àli mouhammadine »

O Allaah, send prayers upon Muhammad and upon the family of Muhammad,

كما صليت على إبراهيم و على آل إبراهيم

« Kamà sallayeta alà ibrahiim wa alà àli ibrahim »

as You sent prayers upon Ibraaheem and the family of Ibraaheem,

وبارك على محمد و على آل محمد

« Wa bàrik alà mouhammadine wa alà àli mouhammadine »

O Allaah, bless Muhammad and the family of Muhammad

كما باركت على إبراهيم و على آل إبراهيم

« Kamà bàrakta alà ibrahim wa alà àli ibrahim »

as You blessed Ibraaheem and the family of Ibraaheem,

.في العالمين إنك حميد مجيد

« fi l-a-alamina innaka hamidoune majide »

You are indeed Worthy of Praise, Full of Glory.

The termination of the prayers takes place as follows:

The head is turned to the right and you say:

السلام عليكم و رحمة الله تعالى و بركاته

"As-salàmou a-alaykoum wa rahmatou-llàhi
ta-alà wa barakàtouh"

Peace, mercy and blessings of Almighty God

Then the head is turned to the left and you say:

السلام عليكم و رحمة الله تعالى و بركاته
"As-salàmou alaykoum wa rahmato llàhi
ta-alà wa barakàtouh"

Peace, mercy and blessings of Almighty God

After finishing your prayer, SALAH ADDUHER, you can say your « Dua »

اللهم إني أسألك برحمتك التي وسعت كل شي أن تغفر لي

« Allàhoumma inni as-alouka birahmatika allati
wasi-ate koula shaye-ine ane taghfira lii »

O Allaah , I ask you by your mercy which envelopes
all things , that you forgive me .

ABLUTION

IN ISLAM

From page n° 54 till page n° 66

ABLUTION IN ISLAM

Of course, if you want to pray, you should keep yourself in state of clean and pure. And so as to be so, you have to perform ablution.

"Prayer without ablution is invalid »

Indeed, ablution « ALWOUDOU » is an islamic procedure for cleansing the whole body or parts of it. The ablution is normally done in preparation for formal daily five obligatory prayers or before handling and reading the Quran.

There are three types of ablution:

1/ Partial ablution: washing parts of the body using water. This type of ablution is an acte for purifying some activities such as urination, defecation, flatulence, deep sleep, light bleeding. This ablution is perfomed everyday.

2/ Dry ablution: « Attayamoume »: replacing water with stone or sand when there is no water.

3/ Full ablution: washing the whole body using water after sexual intercourse, childbirth or menstruation. This involves similar steps to the above (1rst ablution), with the addition of rinsing the left and right sides of the body as well.

In this part, we will present for you how you can perfom islamic partial ablution step by step so as to practice your daily prayers correctly.

So, when someone determines to cleanse oneself for prayer, for the sake of Allah. Then, one begins with :

بِإِسْمِ اللهِ الرحمان الرحيم
« bismillahi rra7maani rra7iime »
In the name of Allah, Most Gracious, Most Merciful.

And with water, one then begins to wash some parts of one's body as follows:

1/ **Wash the hands** three times, making sure that the water reaches between the fingers and all

2/ Wash the mouth three times, bringing a handful of water to the mouth and rinsing thoroughly

3/ Wash the nose three times, using the right hand to bring water up to the nose, sniffing the water, and using the left hand to expel it.

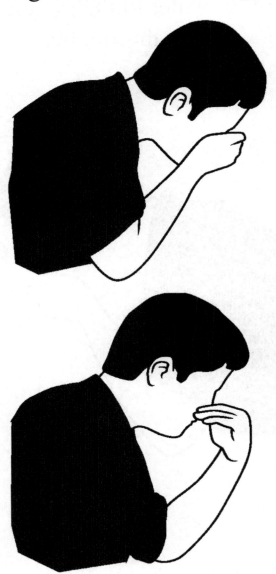

4/ Wash the face three times, from the forehead to the chin and from ear to ear.

5/ Wash the arms three times, up to the elbows, starting with the right arm.

First, the right arm.

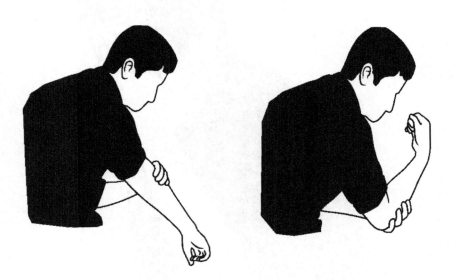

Then, the left arm.

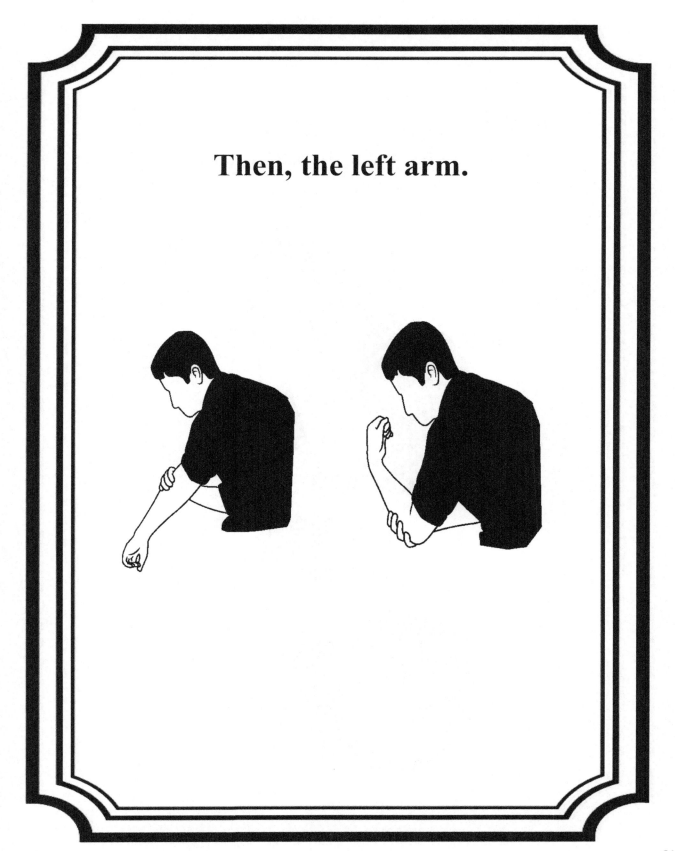

6/ Wash the head one time, using wet hands to wipe over the head from front to back and front again.

7/ Wash the ears one time, using wet fingers to wipe the inside and outside of the ears.

8/ Wash the feet three times, up to the ankles, starting with the right.

So, first the right foot.

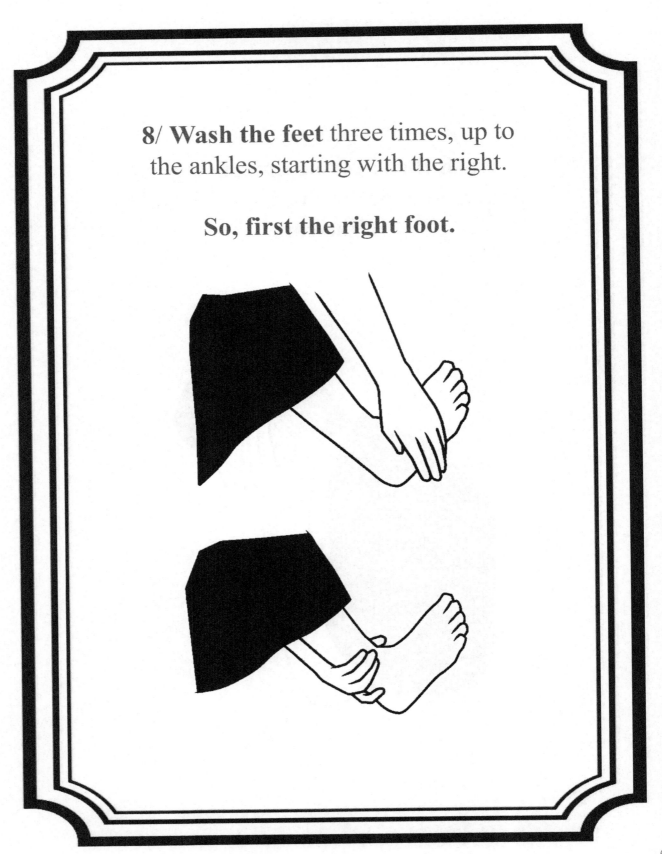

Then, wash the left foot.

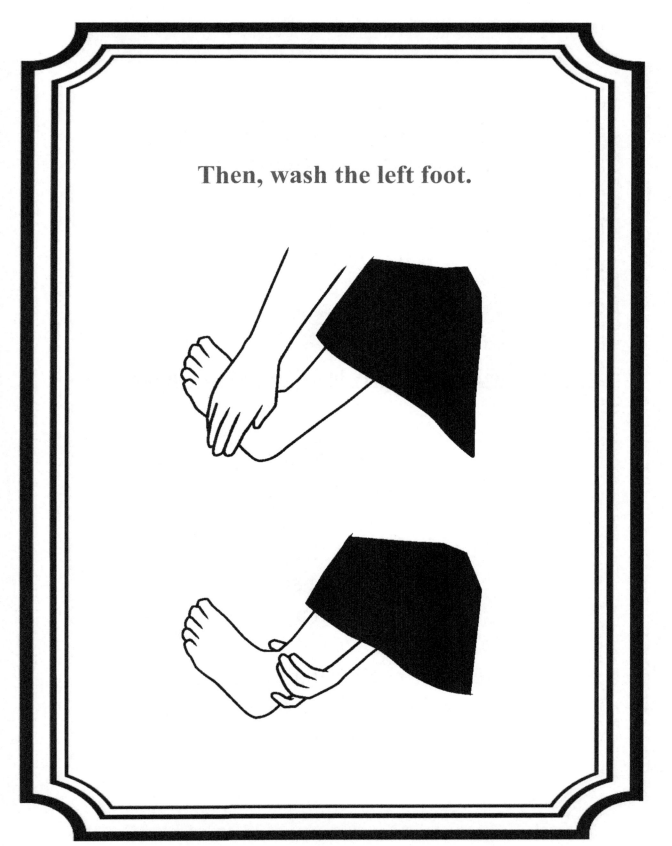

It's very important to mention that
before each everyday prayer,
the muslim person does not need
to repeat the ablution « al wudu »
if it is not broken.

* * * * *

And the actions that may break the ablution include:

- Urination;
- Defecation;
- Flatulence;
- Deep sleep;
Falling unconscious;
Bleeding from a wound.

Of course, after each urination or defecation,
the parts involved are to be washed
before the ablution.

الحمد لله ربي العالمين

« Alhamdou lilàhi rabbi l-a-alamine »

Praise be to Allah, the Cherisher and Sustainer of the worlds.

COPY RIGHT 2020 BY TAMOH ART PUBLISHING
ALL RIGHTS SERVICES ARE RESERVED

Printed in Great Britain
by Amazon

38114873R00037